SHEFFIELD
PAST & PRESENT

A boot black plying his trade, *c.* 1910, outside the former new post office building, situated at the corner of Haymarket and Commercial Street. It opened in 1871 and replaced a building in Market Place. It ceased to be used as a post office in 1910 when its business was transferred to premises which had been built in Flat Street. The Sheffield Stock Exchange occupied part of the building until 1967 and the Yorkshire Penny Bank (now Yorkshire Bank) opened a branch in the building in the 1920s, from where it is still operating. The building which juts out into Commercial Street, with the pedimented window, is the offices and showroom of the Sheffield United Gas Light Company. (*David J. Richardson Collection*)

SHEFFIELD
PAST & PRESENT

GEOFFREY HOWSE

SUTTON PUBLISHING

First published in the United Kingdom in 2000 by Sutton Publishing Limited

This new paperback edition first published in 2007 by
Sutton Publishing, an imprint of NPI Media Group
Cirencester Road · Chalford · Stroud · Gloucestershire · GL6 8PE

British Library Cataloguing in Publication Data
A catalogue record for this book is available from the British Library.

ISBN 978-0-7509-4895-1

Front endpaper: The Royal Hospital, West Street, 1925. (*David J. Richardson Collection*)

Back endpaper: West Street, July 2000. (*Paul T. Langley Welch*)

Half title page: Castle Hill in 1915, looking towards Waingate. This was one of many streets in the labyrinth which occupied the site of Sheffield Castle. The site is now covered by Castle Market. (*David J. Richardson Collection*)

Title page: Sheffield City Hall and Barker's Pool form the focal point of this aerial view, taken in 1938. (*David J. Richardson Collection*)

Typeset in Photina.
Typesetting and origination by
Sutton Publishing.
Printed and bound in England.

Contents

A frozen River Don in 1898. The curved building to the left of Lady's Bridge is the Lady's Bridge Hotel, which was built in 1852 and attached to Tennant Brothers Exchange Brewery. (*David J. Richardson Collection*)

Sheffield: An Introduction

Sheffield has for centuries enjoyed an enviable world-wide reputation for the high quality manufacturing industries on which the city has developed. Its cutlery industry was first mentioned in Geoffrey Chaucer's *Canterbury Tales* (*c.* 1340–1400), when at the beginning of 'The Reeves Tale',. Chaucer mentions 'A Sheffield thwitel [whittler] barr he in his hose'. Sheffield has remained the world leader in the cutlery industry and, from the late seventeenth century onwards, it also became the most famous area for the production of high quality steel in the world. As the area evolved into the modern city we know today many changes have taken place. With few exceptions the oldest buildings to survive intact in the city centre date from the early Georgian period although many street names stand as reminders of Sheffield's medieval past.

Unfortunately the finest surviving examples of medieval buildings were situated around the site of Sheffield's ancient castle and their remains lie buried beneath the modern Castle Market. In other parts of Sheffield, large numbers of medieval buildings were torn down during the eighteenth, nineteenth and early twentieth centuries.

In his *A Tour through the Whole Island of Great Britain* (1724–26), Daniel Defoe writes of Sheffield: 'The town of Sheffield is very populous and large, the streets narrow, and the houses dark and black, occasioned by the continued smoke of the forges, which are always at work'. In 1736, not long after Defoe's visit, the population was 10,121, with a further 4,410 people living within the rural parts which comprised the extensive parish of Sheffield. At that time, when one compares the population of other towns and cities, Sheffield would indeed have been considered large, as the entire population of England amounted to less than six million people. London had for the time, an enormous population of half a million but the next largest city, Norwich, had a population of around 30,000 people. So Sheffield, although still a town, and with an ever increasing population, soon overtook many cities and county towns in size. The parish of Sheffield was incorporated as the borough of Sheffield in 1843 and the town was granted a City Charter in 1893. At the beginning of the twenty-first century Sheffield has a population of over half a million.

The growth of Sheffield and its industrial expansion was largely due to its geographical location. Like Rome, Sheffield is built on seven hills. It was, however, not its hills which made Sheffield a great industrial centre but its water supply. Sheffield is blessed with five river valleys, the rivers being the Don, Loxley, Porter, Rivelin and Sheaf. The plentiful supply of water, combined with the rich beds of iron ore and ample timber available locally, hastened the development of the iron and steel industries. Scores of dams were built in the river valleys to hold water to turn hundreds of water wheels. Timber was turned into charcoal for the smelting and forging industries, making Sheffield a great centre of industry long before the Industrial Revolution, after which coal became the main source of power for Sheffield's industries.

By the time of the first official census in 1801 the population of the parish of Sheffield had risen to 45,755, of whom 31,314 resided within the central township. Rapid expansion continued and fifty years

One of several triumphal arches which were erected in Broomhill for the visit of their Royal Highnesses the Prince and Princess of Wales in 1875, when they opened Broomhill Park. (*David J. Richardson Collection*)

later the population numbered 135,310 inhabitants. This increase in population resulted in extensive building throughout Sheffield. In the centre, the changes to Sheffield's buildings have been more concentrated. The houses which once proliferated in central Sheffield during the eighteenth, nineteenth and early twentieth centuries have largely disappeared, as more and more people have moved to the suburbs. Buildings have replaced buildings, often several times and often they have left little trace that thriving communities of Sheffielders once lived and worked in the locality. Within present day streets there are, however, some reminders of the city's past and within these pages the dramatic changes which have taken place are clearly illustrated.

It was during the reign of Queen Victoria that the foundations of the Sheffield we know today were laid. During that period a commercial quarter was created in the central area and the township was extended westwards, north-westwards and eastwards as new middle-class estates and working-class suburbs were developed, far beyond the boundaries of the ancient township. In the eastern portion immigrants came from elsewhere in Yorkshire, some from Derbyshire and smaller numbers from Nottinghamshire, Leicestershire and various other English counties, where they soon filled the terraces which had been built to accommodate the new workforce. Some immigrants came from Ireland and settled mostly in the north-western quarter of central Sheffield. A few people came from Scotland and even fewer from Wales. There were also some German immigrants during this period.

During the second half of the nineteenth century the steel industry surpassed cutlery making as the area's major industry. The need for high quality steel for railways, ship-building and armaments meant that the Sheffield steel barons no longer looked to the cutlery industry as their major customers. Although industry in Sheffield was booming, the down side was that the concentration of heavy industry resulted in the townscape changing dramatically and, some residents thought, unfavourably. Large numbers of Sheffielders connected with the cutlery industry emigrated, particularly to the United States of America, where they became employed in the cutlery industry there. Some returned but many former Sheffield families settled permanently overseas. During the second half of the twentieth century, industrial production methods changed and hundreds of acres of steelworks and factory buildings were demolished as they became surplus to requirements. So did the workforce. Thousands became unemployed. At first the recovery was slow but Sheffield remains a forward thinking city and expansion has taken place in other areas, providing diverse forms of employment. Sheffield still remains the world leader in the cutlery and steel industries. Modern production methods mean that considerably fewer people work in these industries today, yet although the steel industry

The Sheffield Horse and Carriage Repository, *c.* 1895, situated between Waingate and Exchange Street where Castle Market now stands. (*David J. Richardson Collection*)

employs less than 10 per cent of the workforce it did in the early twentieth century, more tons of steel are currently being produced in Sheffield than at any time during its history.

Sheffield is England's fourth largest city. It is also the greenest and is situated right at the centre of Britain. Over 9,000,000 people live within an hour's drive of the city – 20,000,000 within two hours' drive. East Midlands and Manchester international airports are within easy reach and, since 1977, Sheffield City Airport has provided a useful business link to other UK airports and to Europe's capital cities. Sheffield was the first city to be designated a National City of Sport by the Sports Council of Great Britain. In 1998 the National Centre for Popular Music opened. With a student population of over 45,000 and two universities, Sheffield has become a centre of educational excellence. Increasingly becoming a favourite conference and meeting location, each year the universities are host to over 75,000 conference delegates. The closing years of the twentieth century saw a major transformation of the city of Sheffield, never more dramatically illustrated than during the 1990s.

In the pages of this book I have tried to capture the diversity of change in Sheffield, which has taken place over more than a hundred years. I have concentrated on geographical areas which will perhaps be the most familiar as it is in the centre of Sheffield that the major changes have taken place. There are many aspects which I have not been able to cover in detail. For instance, Sheffield's breweries, which were numerous, the considerable number of hotels, inns, and public houses, (no less than 1,500 licensed premises according to the 1831 census, in the Sheffield district, yet it was still a comparatively small area); transport, in particular the tram, firstly horse drawn, then mechanised, their extinction in October 1960 and their resurrection in the form of the Supertram in May 1994; Sheffield's superb medical facilities, its schools, colleges and two universities; its art galleries, museums, historic houses and its great sporting heritage. Sheffield is crammed full of history. There are so many avenues to explore, which could run to scores of volumes, as every street has its own story to tell. If only the stones could speak.

Sheffield veterinary surgeon Mr Abson and his family, in their Stanley steam car in 1910. (*David J. Richardson Collection*)

I have looked for images of old Sheffield which have not been widely used and, at the same time, I have attempted to include the areas of central Sheffield which will be familiar to most people. As this great city continues to develop, no doubt the diversity of the activities will stamp their own memories and legacies on the historic map of the city, for future generations to enjoy.

This photograph of Moorhead was taken by J.H. Turner in 1958. On 17 May 1958, Her Majesty Queen Elizabeth the Queen Mother visited Sheffield. Trams were diverted from the front of the Town Hall onto little used sections of track. (*David J. Richardson Collection*)

The High Street Area

Pavement artists outside Fitzalan Market, High Street 1903.
(*David J. Richardson Collection*)

High Street, 1863, taken from Sheffield parish church. One of Sheffield's oldest streets, the High Street was originally a link between the medieval castle and the church. Parts of High Street were only 20 feet wide. In the closing years of the nineteenth century the street was widened and many buildings were demolished. (*David J. Richardson Collection*)

High Street, 1892. This view was taken from just below the parish church at the corner of Fargate. (*David J. Richardson Collection*)

A late nineteenth century view of High Street taken from a similar spot to the previous photograph, shortly before the street was widened. W. Foster & Son, whose advertising sign boasts that they are the 'Oldest Clothiers in the City' is at No. 8 High Street and W. Lewis's tobacconists is at No. 6. (*David J. Richardson Collection*)

High Street taken from Cole's Corner at the bottom of Fargate, 1936. The Sheffield Telegraph building on the north side of the street was built in 1913. (*David J. Richardson Collection*)

High Street taken from a similar viewing point in July 2000. (*Paul T. Langley Welch*)

High Street 1905. Looking up the street towards Cole's Corner and Cutlers' Hall in Church Street. (*David J. Richardson Collection*)

High Street, 12 July 1905. Walsh's store is decorated for the visit of their Majesties King Edward Vll and Queen Alexandra for the opening of Sheffield University. John Walsh opened his store in 1896. It suffered severe bomb damage during Sheffield Blitz in December 1940. Walsh's then transferred to temporary premises in The Mount until they moved to their newly built High Street premises, on the site of their old store in 1953. In the 1970s Walsh's became Rackhams, in the 1980s House of Fraser and after its closure in the 1990s it was taken over by T.J. Hughes. (*David J. Richardson Collection*)

High Street from a similar viewing point to the previous photograph, in July 2000. (*Paul T. Langley Welch*)

Fitzalan Market, 1905. Situated at the top of Angel Street, at its Junction with High Street. The area to the front of the building on the Angel Street side was known as Market Place. The horse and cart is crossing High Street from Fitzalan Square. Fitzalan Market opened in 1786, the original building being replaced by the one seen here in 1864. This market specialised in meat and fish. The corn market was held each Tuesday on the High Street side. The building closed on 24 April 1930 and was demolished in 1931. (*David J. Richardson Collection*)

The site of Fitzalan Market today. (*Paul T. Langley Welch*)

The bottom end of
the Fitzalan Market
building at the junction
of Haymarket and
High Street in 1905
(the section around
the corner to the left
in High Street being
shown as Fruit Market
on the 1890 map of
the area). The building
curves round to the
right into King Street.
On the corner is Dean &
Dawson, Tourist Agents.
(*David J. Richardson
Collection*)

The same site as the previous photograph in 2000. (*Paul T. Langley Welch*)

The bottom end of the King Street side of the Fitzalan Market building, 1920. Among the advertisements at Dean and Dawson's, several can be seen for the White Star Line liner *Olympic*, sister ship of the ill-fated *Titanic*. (*David J. Richardson Collection*)

The bottom end of King Street today, showing the site of the former premises of Dean & Dawson. (*Paul T. Langley Welch*)

King Street from Market Place/Angel Street looking towards Haymarket in 1898. In medieval times this street was known as Pudding Lane. (*David J. Richardson Collection*)

King Street as it appears in 2000. (*Paul T. Langley Welch*)

Castle Square as it appeared from 1967 until 1994, when the 'hole in the road', seen here, provided access at basement level to a number of shops and department stores. The reintroduction of trams to the streets of central Sheffield necessitated the filling-in of this popular – although somewhat briefly lived – Sheffield landmark. The cinema which can be seen in Fitzalan Square opened in 1911, as the Electra Palace, and was the first Sheffield cinema to offer continuous performances. The building was destroyed by fire in 1984. This view was taken in 1973 by T.R. Arkell. (*SCL Collection*)

A view taken by T.R. Arkell in 1973 of Castle Square, looking up the High Street. Walsh's department store can be seen on the left. The Midland Bank on the corner of High Street and Angel Street is now a public house known as the Bankers Draft. (*SCL Collection*)

Angel Street/ Market Place 1895, as seen from what is now Castle Square. (*David J. Richardson Collection*)

Angel Street taken from the same viewing point as the previous photograph, 2000. (*Paul T. Langley Welch*)

Haymarkct in 1979. A 'Bendy Bus', one of Sheffield's popular sights for over two decades can be seen in the left foreground. (*David J. Richardson Collection*)

Haymarket, July 2000. Kings Street can be seen in the left foreground. (*Paul T. Langley Welch*)

Cockayne's store at no. 1 Angel Street 1900. The store was founded by two brothers, Thomas B. and William Cockayne as a general drapers. The firm expanded and during the twentieth century the five storey shop seen here was selling a wide range of goods. Cockayne's store was destroyed in December 1940 during the Sheffield Blitz. (*David J. Richardson Collection*)

The same site in July 2000. Cockayne's traded from their new store after the Second World War, until the shop was taken over by Schofield's. The entire premises are now occupied by the Argos Superstore. (*Paul T. Langley Welch*)

Castle Street, *c. 1895*. Castle Street runs from the bottom of Angel Street to the junction of Haymarket and Waingate, the site of Sheffield's ancient castle. Jones' Sewing Machine Company Ltd stands next to Naylor's Confectioners. Next to Naylor's, the building with the arched windows is the Empire Mantle Company Ltd. beyond which is the Temperance Hotel. (*SCL Collection*)

Castle Street, July 2000. Many of the buildings seen in the previous photograph have been demolished. The mural on the gable end of the former premises of the Empire Mantle Company, serves as a reminder of the importance of the steel industry to Sheffield. The artist was Paul Waplington. The mural was painted 1986 and is titled 'Steelworker' (*Paul T. Langley Welch*)

An engraving of the Tontine Hotel, 1830. (*David J. Richardson Collection*)

The Norfolk Market Hall, *c.* 1900. The Norfolk Market Hall stood on the site of the Tontine Hotel and a brewery. The Duke of Norfolk purchased the Tontine Hotel and the adjacent brewery from Tennant brothers and promptly pulled both buildings down. He then spent £30,000 building his new market hall. It measured 296 ft x 115 ft x 45 ft high and opened in time for Christmas shopping in December 1851. The Duke of Norfolk owned extensive estates in and around Sheffield. He also had the rights to all the markets in Sheffield. These rights were purchased from the Duke by Sheffield Corporation in 1899 for £526,000. When Castle Market opened in 1959, the Norfolk Market Hall closed. It was demolished in November 1960. (*SCL Collection*)

Wilkinson's store, site of the Norfolk Market Hall, July 2000, seen from the edge of Fitzalan Square. Wilkinson's is situated just past the East Gate pedestrian bridge, across Dixon Lane. Commercial Street is in the right foreground, High Street in the left. (*Paul T. Langley Welch*)

Waingate, 1915. The premises of Lenton & Rusby who were spectacle makers and were established in Waingate in 1817. They were a noted manufacturer of spectacle frames and lenses and exported their products throughout Britain and to various European countries. The gable to the right belongs to the Royal Hotel, which opened in 1783 as the Reindeer Inn. The entire site was destroyed in December 1940, during the Sheffield Blitz. (*David J. Richardson Collection*)

Waingate, July 2000. A branch of the opticians, Dolland & Aitchison, are operating from the site of Lenton & Rusby. (*Paul T. Langley Welch*)

Around the Site of Sheffield Castle

A barrow girl in Sheaf Street, *c.* 1905. (*David J. Richardson Collection*)

The site of Sheffield Castle, as seen in July 2000. This large castle extended from the present Waingate to the area bounded by the River Sheaf, covering the site now occupied by Castle Market. There were Anglo-Danish buildings on the site, before the Norman Conquests. The Normans were quick to realise the strategic importance of the site, on which they chose to construct their castle. Sheffield Castle was completely destroyed in 1649-50, when Parliament ordered that all castles which had been fortified by the Royalists during the Civil War should be demolished. (*Paul T. Langley Welch*)

Sheffield old Town Hall, Waingate, July 2000. Sheffield's earliest town hall stood by the church gates in High Street. It was replaced in 1808 by the building seen here on the right side of Waingate, with its tower and clock. When the present town hall was completed it became the Court House. (*Paul T. Langley Welch*)

Lady's Bridge, 1915. This bridge was the terminus for trams running on the Brightside and Tinsley route. The bridge has ancient origins and gets its name from the chantry chapel which stood on an earlier bridge on the same site. The chantry chapel was destroyed in the sixteenth century, at the time of the dissolution of the monasteries. (*David J. Richardson Collection*)

Lady's Bridge, July 2000. The Lady's Bridge Hotel is standing empty. Scaffolding has been erected as work to refurbish the premises gets under way. The former pub and adjacent brewery are being converted into flats and offices. (*Paul T. Langley Welch*)

Lady's Bridge, 1909, looking from the direction of Blonk Street Bridge. The Lady's Bridge Hotel seen on the left of the bridge was opened in 1852 and was attached to Tennant Brothers Exchange Brewery, whose buildings and chimneys can be seen behind. Tennants had moved there after the Duke of Norfolk had purchased their previous brewery in order to build his market hall. (*David J. Richardson Collection*)

Lady's Bridge in the present day. The extensive alterations which took place to Exchange Street, Furnival Road and Blonk Street, in the early 1930s, prevent an exact comparison photograph being taken. (*Paul T. Langley Welch*)

Blonk Street Bridge, 1898. The large building on the right skyline is the Alexandra Theatre and Opera House. On the right beyond the projecting wall can be seen the River Sheaf at its confluence with the River Don. (*David J. Richardson Collection*)

Blonk Street Bridge, July 2000. The major alterations to the Exchange Street area in the 1930s have completely changed the view. The theatre has gone and there is a road where it once stood. The Alexandra Hotel on the right, occupies part of the site of the theatre although it has been set back beyond the original building line. The River Sheaf has been culverted and it can be glimpsed emerging into the River Don from the arch to the right of the old public lavatories, which stand on the right of Blonk Street Bridge. (*Paul T. Langley Welch*)

Wicker Arches, July 1905. The Wicker and Wicker Arches have been decorated for the royal visit. The Wicker entrance to Victoria Station is on the left of the arches. The Lord Mayor of Sheffield, Herbert Hughes, can be seen wearing his mayoral robes, in the left foreground. The origins of the name Wicker could lie in the old Norse word 'vikir', which means willow and 'carr' or 'kerr' a broad flat meadow. The Wicker was once meadowland and it lies close to the River Don which, until its banks were crowded by breweries and steelworks, may well have been fringed with willow trees. (*David J. Richardson Collection*)

Wicker Arches, July 2000. The arches are substantially cleaner than they were at the beginning of the twentieth century, when steam trains crossed them and the soot from the surrounding heavy industries covered the stonework with a layer of grime. (*Paul T. Langley Welch*)

Spital Hill, 1935. So called because in the twelfth century William de Lovetot, Lord of Hallamshire, founded an isolation hospital, the Hospital of St. Leonard. It existed until the reign of Henry VIII. Its site is commemorated in the name Spital Hill. The entrance to the L.M.S. Goods Yard can be seen on the right of the photograph. (*David J. Richardson Collection*)

Spital Hill, July 2000. Motor car showrooms occupy part of the site of what was once the L.M.S. Goods Yard. (*Paul T. Langley Welch*)

The Shambles, *c.* 1910. More commonly known as the 'Killing Shambles', they were slaughter houses situated on the site of Sheffield Castle, and had been moved to that site at the end of the eighteenth century, having previously been situated in the High Street. The gully running down the centre of the cobbled alley was where the unwanted fluids from slaughtered animals were swilled. Over the wall at the bottom is the River Sheaf. The gable end of the backstage area of the Alexandra Theatre and Opera House, can be seen. The backstage area was built out over the river on stilts and was notoriously cold. (*David J. Richardson Collection*)

Blonk Street, *c.* 1900. On the left is the Victoria Hotel, situated in Furnival Road and on the right the Alexandra Theatre and Opera House built in 1836. Originally called the Adelphi, it was renamed the Alexandra Music Hall in 1865 and was situated at the confluence of the River Sheaf and River Don. The stage was, reputedly, the largest in the provinces. During its latter years, the theatre was commonly referred to as the 'Old Alec'. In 1914 it was purchased by Sheffield Corporation and demolished in order to carry out a street improvement programme. The First World War intervened. Plans were shelved and the scheme eventually went ahead in the 1930s. (*SCL Collection*)

This view, taken in July 2000, is from the same spot as the previous photograph. The Alexandra Hotel is situated on a small part of the site of the theatre, which stood where the cars are seen travelling along Blonk Street, towards Park Square. (*Paul T. Langley Welch*)

The Victoria Hotel, Furnival Road, 1905. The Alexandra Theatre & Opera House is on the right of the photograph. (*David J. Richardson Collection*)

The site of the Victoria Hotel in July 2000. (*Paul T. Langley Welch*)

The corner of Exchange Street and
Furnival Road, *c.* 1905. (*SCL Collection*)

Exchange Street from Furnival Road,
c. 1905. (*SCL Collection*)

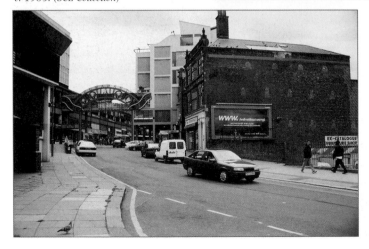

Exchange Street in July 2000, looking
towards Haymarket. (*Paul T. Langley Welch*)

Broad Street, c. 1890, which later became engulfed by the 'Rag & Tag'. A wholesale Fish Market opened on Shude Hill in 1879. By the middle of the decade that followed, the area adjacent to it was being used as an open air market selling a wider range of goods. Known officially as Sheaf Market but to generations of Sheffielders as the 'Rag & Tag', it was a crowded and very popular area. The 'Rag & Tag' closed in March 1973 and its trade transferred to the new Sheaf Market, built on the site of the old Castlefolds Market. (*David J. Richardson Collection*)

A view from the roof of the Pheasant Inn, Broad Street (the Pheasant Inn is featured in the previous photograph) across the rooftops to the Corn Exchange, c. 1890. (*David J. Richardson Collection*).

Sheaf Street in 1952, showing the Corn Exchange. It was built on the site of the Shrewsbury Hospital by the Duke of Norfolk in 1881. It not only provided premises for corn dealers but was the offices of the Duke's Sheffield estates. It also contained several shop units. The building was extensively damaged by fire in 1947. It never re-opened and was finally demolished in 1964. (*David J. Richardson Collection*)

A view of Exchange Street, *c.* 1905, taken from the roof of the Corn Exchange. The tower and clock of the old Town Hall in Waingate can be seen on the extreme left skyline. (*David J. Richardson Collection*)

Part of the 'Rag & Tag' in 1964. (*David J. Richardson Collection*)

The site of the buildings in the previous photograph in July 2000. (*Paul T. Langley Welch*)

Park Square, July 2000.
The site of the Corn Exchange.
(*Paul T. Langley Welch*)

Sheffield canal basin, 1989. Construction of Sheffield Ship Canal commenced in 1815. The canal opened on 22 February 1819 and served Sheffield's industries for over a hundred years. This view shows the sad state of dilapidation the once thriving canal basin had reached by the end of the 1980s. (*SCL Collection*)

Sheffield canal basin in July 2000. The canal basin was restored by Sheffield City Council which spent £10 million on the project in the early 1990s. Renamed Victoria Quays, the old canal basin is one of the most attractive features in the city centre. (*Paul T. Langley Welch*)

Midland railway station, 14 May 1965.
(*SCL Collection*)

Midland railway station in August 1983,
after the cleaning of the façade.
(*SCL Collection*)

Midland railway station, July 2000.
(*Paul T. Langley Welch*)

This photograph, taken by J.H. Turner, shows Midland railway station in 1956. (*David J. Richardson Collection*)

Midland railway station in July 2000. (*Paul T. Langley Welch*)

A view across the rooftops towards Midland station, 1928. (*David J. Richardson Collection*)

Another 1928 view shows the magnificent countryside which lies just beyond the industrial city. (*David J. Richardson Collection*)

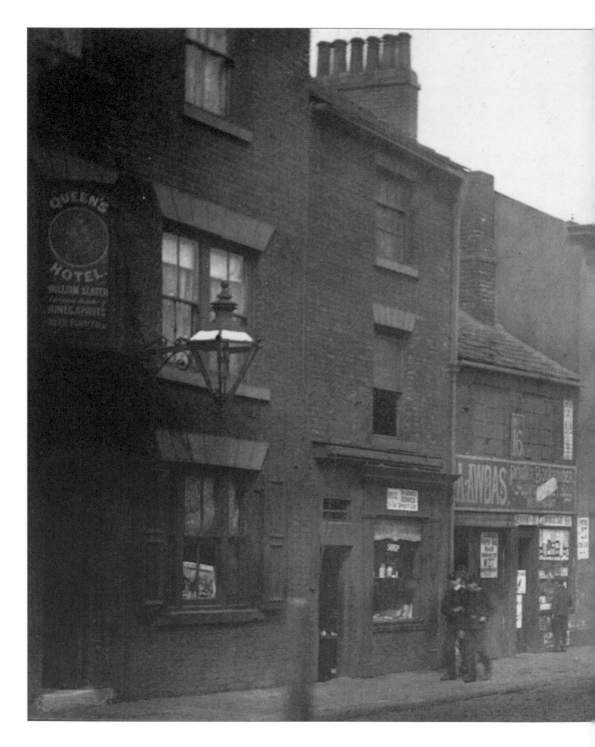

Sheaf Street, *c.* 1890. Smoke from the smoke stack of a train in Midland Station can be seen on the extreme right of the buildings, above the head of the driver of the horse and dray. (*David J. Richardson Collection*)

A present day view from Arundel Gate past Midland Station to Hyde Park flats. (*Paul T. Langley Welch*)

Around Fargate

The Music Hall, Surrey Street, photographed by W.H. Babington, *c.* 1900. Built in 1823, to the design of architects J.G. Weightman and M.E. Hadfield, it opened the following year. It presented diverse high quality entertainment, featuring such artistes as Paganini and Jenny Lind. Charles Dickens also appeared there. It became a warehouse in 1902 before it was taken over by the public library service. It was demolished in the early 1930s. The Central Library and Graves Art Gallery were built on the site. (*SCL Collection*)

A 1950s view of the Central Library and Graves Art Gallery in Surrey Street, which occupies the site of the Music Hall. The buildings to the right are the Methodist Chapel and the former Surrey Street Medical School, founded in 1828, which moved to Leopold Street in 1888. (*David J. Richardson Collection*)

The Central Library and Graves Art Gallery building in July 2000. (*Paul T. Langley Welch*)

The disastrous fire which rendered the Theatre Royal beyond repair, 30 December 1935. This historic theatre opened in 1773 and was altered several times, having been almost completely rebuilt in 1855, with further alterations being carried out in 1901 by Frank Matcham. (*David J. Richardson Collection*)

This view, taken in 1937, shows the corner of the Lyceum Theatre and the burned out shell of the Theatre Royal. The Lyceum Theatre was built on the site of the City Theatre and Circus which burned down in 1893. Built by the architect W.G.R. Sprague (1865-1933), who was responsible for creating some of the most beautiful theatres in London, including Wyndham's Theatre and The New Theatre (now called Albery). Surprisingly, although Sprague has more theatres still standing in London than any other architect, Sheffield's Lyceum is his only remaining theatre outside the capital. It opened in October 1897. During the 1970s and '80s it was used mostly for bingo but in 1989 work commenced on the restoration of this glorious theatre and the complete rebuilding of the backstage area. (*David J. Richardson Collection*)

A view taken in July 2000 from a similar viewing point to the previous photograph. Part of the Crucible Theatre, Sheffield's famous repertory theatre, can be seen on the right. (*Paul T. Langley Welch*)

Norfolk Street, 1910. The building in the right foreground is St. Marie's Presbytery. The Surrey Street corner of Sheffield Town Hall can be seen at the end of the street. (*David J. Richardson Collection*)

A similar view of Norfolk Street in July 2000. (*Paul T. Langley Welch*)

A view of the opposite side of Norfolk Street to the previous two photographs, taken in 1933. (*David J. Richardson Collection*)

The same site as the previous photograph in July 2000. The Crucible Theatre occupies the site today. It opened in 1971 as a replacement for the Sheffield Playhouse. It has seating for 1,200 patrons and has a thrust stage. It not only houses one of England's finest repertory companies but has achieved worldwide fame for hosting the World Snooker Championships. (*Paul T. Langley Welch*)

Sycamore Street, 1930, shown from its junction with Arundel Street, is one of Sheffield's vanished commercial areas. Part of the Electro Works building can be seen on the right. Sycamore Street ran parallel to Norfolk Street. Part of the site is covered by the Crucible Theatre. (*David J. Richardson Collection*)

Joseph Rodgers Cutlery Works moved to no. 6 Norfolk Street in about 1780. The firm originally produced penknives but, by the time Joseph Rodgers died in 1821 (the year Joseph Rodgers & Sons was granted a royal warrant), leaving his four sons to run the business, the factory was producing cutlery, razors and scissors. The firm's trade mark of the six-pointed star and maltese cross became famous the world over. When advertising their wares, Rodgers' advertising slogan ran 'The King of knives and the knife of Kings'. This is a late nineteenth-century view of Joseph Rodgers & Sons first cutlery showroom, which opened in 1821. (*SCL Collection*)

A view of Pond Street in 1973. (*SCL Collection*)

Pond Street in July 2000 from the same viewpoint. (*Paul T. Langley Welch*)

Chapel Walk, 1952. This attractive shopping street was one of the city centre's 'quaint' shopping areas. (*SCL Collection*)

Chapel Walk as it appears in July 2000. It is a pity that, although the majority of the older buildings remain, unsympathetic and uninspired shop fronts mar what could otherwise be a highly desirable feature of modern Sheffield. (*Paul T. Langley Welch*)

Fargate and Leopold Street, 1900, taken from the junction of Pinstone Street and Barker's Pool. (*David J. Richardson Collection*)

The imposing premises at no. 9, Fargate, *c.* 1950, when it was occupied by Austin Reed. Although it has a narrow principal façade, the building is very large, extending backwards. Black Swan Walk runs from Fargate down the left-hand side of the building and Chapel Walk runs from Fargate down the right-hand side. The building was formerly the premises of A.H. Holland, a firm established in Sheffield in 1844. The building seen here was erected in 1892. Although it was designed by the architects Flockton and Gibbs, Mr Alwyn H. Holland had a say in its design. He was a great lover of art and was heavily influenced by John Ruskin and William Morris. Part of this attractive building was given over to the display of paintings and fine pottery. A.H. Holland was a high class provision merchant. The building also housed Holland's Restaurant. The premises are currently occupied by The Link. (*SCL Collection*)

Fargate taken from Cole's Corner, July 2000. Number 9 Fargate, the architecturally important premises, originally occupied by A.H. Holland, can be seen with its incongrous contemporary shop front. The narrow entrance to Black Swan Walk is to the left of The Link and the entrance to Chapel Walk is to the right. (*Paul T. Langley Welch*)

A view from the same
position as that on page 60,
July 2000.
(*Paul T. Langley Welch*)

Cole Brothers Ltd, Fargate, 1963. Cole Brothers was founded by three brothers in 1863. This building, which stood at the bottom of Fargate, was built in the 1860s. Cole's corner was a popular meeting point for the next hundred years. In 1963 Cole Brothers moved to new premises in Barker's Pool. Shortly afterwards, the building seen here was demolished. Cole Brothers is now part of the John Lewis Partnership. (*David J. Richardson Collection*)

Fargate in July 2000. HSBC Bank now occupies the site which was formerly Cole Brothers, as seen in the previous view. Many Sheffielders still refer to the area as Cole's corner. (*Paul T. Langley Welch*)

The south side of Fargate, 1920. Hanbidge's shop is at the junction of Norfolk Row. (*David J. Richardson Collection*)

The south side of Fargate, July 2000. (*Paul T. Langley Welch*)

Fitzalan Square,
1902. The name
is derived from
a branch of the
Howard family,
the family name
of the Dukes of
Norfolk. This
open space was
created in 1881
on the site of
buildings which
were demolished
in Market Street.
The Fitzalan
Market Hall can
be seen across
the square with
Haymarket to
its right. (*David
J. Richardson
Collection*)

Fitzalan Square, July 2000. (*Paul T. Langley Welch*)

Commercial Street viewed from the edge of Fitzalan Square, by the side of Fitzalan Market, 1902. The large building on the corner was opened in 1881 as the Midland Banking Company. It became the United Counties Bank in 1907 and was taken over by Barclays Bank in 1916. The building was demolished in 1969. The building which can be glimpsed on the left of Commercial Street is the offices and showroom of the Sheffield United Gas Light Company. (*David J. Richardson Collection*)

A similar view of the same site in July 2000. (*Paul T. Langley Welch*)

The Cathedral Area

The church of St Peter, Church Street, shortly before the First World War. (*SCL Collection*)

This view, taken from a lantern slide, shows Blue Coat Boys on their way to a service at Sheffield parish church, in 1894. The Blue Coat Boys Charity School was established in 1706, and originally boys were taught in a room in the Shrewsbury Hospital. A school was built in 1710 by public subscription in East Parade. A new larger building opened on the same site in 1825. The school could accommodate 100 fatherless or orphaned boys. The uniform consisted of blue coats with brass buttons and yellow braid, green corduroy trousers and a blue cap. The school transferred to a new building in Psalter Lane in 1911 and survived until the Second World War. The boys were evacuated and the school buildings requisitioned. The Blue Coat Boys Charity School never reopened. (*David J. Richardson Collection*)

A view of the Cathedral Church of St Peter and St Paul, taken in July 2000, from the same spot as the previous photograph. (*Paul T. Langley Welch*)

Townhead Street, *c.* 1902. The properties at the bottom of the street had become a notorious slum area and major clearance took place. (*SCL Collection*)

Townhead Street, July 1972. (*Paul T. Langley Welch*)

71

Looking down Snig Hill, *c.* 1900. (*SCL Collection*)

A similar view of Snig
Hill, July 2000. (*Paul
T. Langley Welch*)

Looking up Snig Hill, *c.* 1900.
(*SCL Collection*)

Looking up Snig Hill from a similar spot
in 1973. (*SCL Collection*)

Snig Hill from a similar viewing point to
the previous two photographs, taken in
July 2000. (*Paul T. Langley Welch*)

Campo Lane, *c.* 1895. Campo Lane is an ancient thoroughfare which originally led to the Town Head, now the junction of Campo Lane and Townhead Street. The street was widened in 1929 which, in the part of Campo Lane seen here, meant the removal of bodies from part of the graveyard of Sheffield Cathedral. (*SCL Collection*)

Campo Lane in July 2000, taken from exactly the same spot as the previous photograph. The work carried out to the boundary wall of the Cathedral, seen on the left, can be detected when the two images are compared. (*Paul T. Langley Welch*)

Campo Lane looking in the opposite direction to the previous two views, *c.* 1900. (*SCL Collection*)

Paradise Square, *c.* 1900. Developed in the 1730s, it became a highly desirable residential area and is Sheffield's only surviving Georgian square. One of its most notable residents was the sculptor Sir Francis Chantrey. As the city became completely engulfed by heavy industry, many residents moved to the suburbs. The square was regularly used for markets and various gatherings and meetings. John Wesley preached in Paradise Square. (*SCL Collection*)

Paradise Square, July 2000. From the mid-nineteenth century this attractive square became a busy commercial centre. Today it is mostly occupied by legal and financial offices. (*Paul T. Langley Welch*)

A view of the Sir Frederick Mappin Building in 1924, part of the University of Sheffield, from St. George's Square. (*David J. Richardson Collection*)

This photograph was taken from the same spot as the previous photograph in July 2000. (*Paul T. Langley Welch*)

St James's Row 1953, looking towards the Cutlers' Hall in Church Street. (*SCL Collection*)

St James's Row,
July 2000. (*Paul T.
Langley Welch*)

Church Street, 1903. On the right is the Cutlers' Hall, the home of the Cutlers' Company. The building seen here was constructed in 1832 to the designs of Samuel Worth and B.B. Taylor and extended in 1881. The Cutlers' Company was incorporated by act of Parliament in 1624, to regulate the cutlery industry. Cole Brothers Fargate store can be seen to the left with High Street beyond. The carriages and cabs in Church Street stand outside the parish church of St Peter, later to become Sheffield's Anglican Cathedral. (*David J. Richardson Collection*)

A view to compare with the previous photograph, taken in July 2000. Cutlers' Hall is substantially unchanged, although its stonework is slightly cleaner. Cole Brothers store has long since disappeared. A supertram makes its way past the cathedral, where once horse drawn cabs and carriages collected their passengers. (*Paul T. Langley Welch*)

The present-day tram stop outside the Cathedral Church of St Peter and St Paul. (*Paul T. Langley Welch*)

WHY WORRY?

WHEN

REMOVING

THOS. W. HART

TAKES ALL RISK

BY ROAD or RAIL.

RING UP NO. 2938.

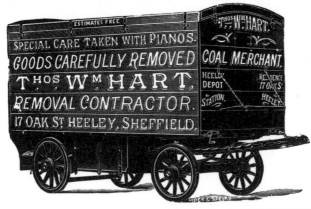

ANY

DESCRIPTION

OF WORK UNDER-

TAKEN WITH

VANS, DRAYS or

CARTS.

Pianos taken through
upper windows.

All risk of breakages
taken.

A 1910 advertisement for the Sheffield removal firm Thomas W. Hart. (*SCL Collection*)

Barker's Pool,
Pinstone Street &
The Moor Area

The Woodman Inn, Ecclesall Road, facing the bottom of the Moor, *c.* 1870. (*David J. Richardson Collection*)

Pinstone Street, *c.* 1850. This photograph was taken before the present town hall was built. (*SCL Collection*)

Pinstone Street from the same viewpoint, July 2000. Sheffield Town Hall is on the left. (*Paul T. Langley Welch*)

Sheffield's growth and ever-increasing population, during the closing years of the nineteenth century, resulted in the building of a more opulent Town Hall than the one in Waingate, which had served Sheffield since 1808. The new Town Hall was designed by E.W. Mountford and built at a cost of £80,000. Building began in 1891 and continued until 1896. It was officially opened by Her Majesty Queen Victoria on 21 May 1897, and is seen here in 1907. (*David J. Richardson Collection*)

Sheffield Town Hall, July 2000. (*Paul T. Langley Welch*)

Barker's Pool, 1907. Named after a Mr Barker who built a reservoir in the vicinity in 1435. The reservoir existed until 1793. The buildings on the right were cleared for the building of the Cinema House, (opened 6 May 1913) and the City Hall (opened 22 September 1932). (*David J. Richardson Collection*)

Barker's Pool in July 2000. (*Paul T. Langley Welch*)

Sheffield City Hall, Barker's Pool. Construction of the hall began in 1930. Until Sheffield Arena was built on the outskirts of Sheffield in the 1990s, the City Hall was the major venue for large concerts, etc. in the area. (*SCL Collection*)

Sheffield City Hall, Barker's Pool, July 2000. (*Paul T. Langley Welch*)

Barker's Pool, 1960. On the right are the steps of the City Hall. The building in the right background, at the corner of Holly Street and Division Street, is the former headquarters of the Sheffield Water Works Company. Cambridge Street can be seen on the left. (*SCL Collection*)

Barker's Pool, July 2000. (*Paul T. Langley Welch*)

Pinstone Street, *c.* 1925. The building in the right foreground is St Paul's Church. (*David J. Richardson Collection*)

Pinstone Street from the same viewpoint. July 2000. The site of St Paul's Church is now occupied the Peace Gardens. (*Paul T. Langley Welch*)

A view from the site of Sheffield Town Hall, during construction in the early 1890s. Norfolk Street can be seen at the rear of the photograph and St Paul's Churchyard is on the right. (*David J. Richardson Collection*)

A view from the site of St Paul's Churchyard looking towards the Town Hall. A reverse view of the previous photograph, Norfolk Street can be seen to the right. The present Peace Gardens, seen here, were created in 1998 and replaced the earlier Peace Gardens created on the site of St Paul's Church and Churchyard after the Second World War, when most of the gravestones were removed. The removal of human remains for burial elsewhere, did not take place until the 1990s. (*Paul T. Langley Welch*)

Moorhead, 1904. The monument was erected on this site in 1863, to the designs of George Goldie and commemorated servicemen who had died in the Crimean War. The column was made of Aberdeen granite, with a stone base and capital. The seated figure which tops the monument represents 'Honour'. The monument was surrounded by iron railings. In this photograph Pinstone Street can be seen to the left and Union Street goes off to the right. The Crimean War Memorial was removed in 1957 to the Botanical Gardens, where it stands today, minus its column. (*David J. Richardson Collection*)

Moorhead, July 2000. The remodelling of the streets makes it impossible to get an exact comparison of the previous view as the creation of Furnival Gate, which now crosses Moorhead, has obliterated the original line of the streets. Furnival Gate goes off to the left and the corner of Cambridge Street can be seen at its junction with Pinstone Street. (*Paul T. Langley Welch*)

The Moor, *c.* 1915, looking towards Moorhead and Pinstone Street. During the twentieth century this was one of Sheffield's busiest shopping thoroughfares, with many department stores. The opening of Meadowhall shopping complex, on the outskirts of Sheffield on Attercliffe Common in September 1990, combined with the opening of other smaller specialist shopping centres elsewhere in Sheffield, has resulted in a decline in The Moor's popularity. Now pedestrianised, this famous Sheffield landmark has been completely transformed. (*SCL Collection*)

The Moor, July 2000, taken from a similar spot to the previous photograph. (*Paul T. Langley Welch*)

Cambridge Street, 1926. Originally called Coal Pit Lane, it once stood at the end of old Sheffield town. It has borne its name since 1857 when His Royal Highness the Duke of Cambridge laid the foundation stone for the Crimean War Memorial, at nearby Moorhead. (*David J. Richardson Collection*)

Cambridge Street seen from the same spot in July 2000. (*Paul T. Langley Welch*)

Cambridge Street, 1963, looking towards Moorhead. On the right, the building with the broken arched pediment is the Hippodrome. Built to the designs of Bertie Crewe, it opened on 23 December 1907, as a variety theatre. It became a cinema in 1931 and was demolished in 1963, shortly after this photograph was taken. (*SCL Collection*)

Cambridge Street, July 2000. The site of the buildings which appear in the previous photograph now forms part of the complex occupied by the Grosvenor House Hotel, whose tower can be seen rising above the lower block on the right. (*Paul T. Langley Welch*)

Looking up Cambridge Street from Pinstone Street in 1973. The site of the Hippodrome is on the left, above the Lotus shoe shop. (*SCL Collection*)

A similar view to that in the previous photograph, July 2000. (*Paul T. Langley Welch*)

93

The corner of Cambridge Street at its junction with Pinstone Street, 1963. (*David J. Richardson Collection*)

The junction of Cambridge Street and Pinstone Street in July 2000. (*Paul T. Langley Welch*)

Union Street in the 1930s, taken from Moorhead. The remodelling of the streets in the area during the deacde that followed, for the creation of Furnival Gate, resulted in the demolition of several buildings, including the Picture Palace, which can also be seen in the photograph below. (*SCL Collection*)

Union Street 1962, looking towards Moorhead. (*David J. Richardson Collection*)

St Paul's Church, Pinstone Street, *c.* 1900. Built by public subscription as a chapel-of-ease, because the nearby Parish Church of St. Peter was rapidly growing short of space, it was considered to be one of Sheffield's finest Georgian buildings. The designs were by Ralph Tunnicliffe of Dalton assisted by the Rotherham architect and master mason John Platt (the elder). The first stone was laid on 28 May 1720 and, although work was completed in 1721, the church remained unused for nineteen years due to a dispute over who should appoint the curate. St Paul's was finally consecrated in 1740. The dome on top of the tower was added in 1769. (*SCL Collection*)

The corner of Pinstone Street in July 2000, showing the site of St Paul's Church and churchyard. Sheffield was an archdeaconry within the diocese of York from 1884. The raising of St Peter's, Sheffield's parish church, to cathedral status in 1914, and the decanting of large numbers of inner city residents to the suburbs, meant that many churches in central Sheffield became redundant. In 1936 it was decided that some churches had to be demolished. The decision to demolish St Paul's, Pinstone Street, has deprived Sheffield of one of its finest buildings. Its close proximity to Sheffield's new cathedral may have been St Paul's downfall. The former parish church of St Peter is now the Cathedral Church of St Peter and St Paul. (*Paul T. Langley Welch*)

The Pinstone Street arch created to form part of the lavish decorations for Her Majesty Queen Vcitoria's visit to Sheffield in 1897. (*SCL Collection*)

Her Majesty Queen Victoria's carriage approaches the steps of Sheffield's new Town Hall, 1897. (*SCL Collection*)

Her Royal Highness the Duchess of York (Later Queen Elizabeth and now Her Majesty Queen Elizabeth the Queen Mother) seen here outside Sheffield Town Hall in 1934 with the Lord Mayor of Sheffield, Percival J.M. Turner, CBE, JP. Her Royal Highness stood in for her husband, who had been taken ill. She opened the city's new central library in Surrey Street during their visit. (*SCL Collection*)

The corner of Ecclesall Road, *c.* 1890. The premises of W.H. Haigh, cab, coach & omnibus proprietor. News Flash! 5 November 1889 – Haigh fined for cruelly working horses on the Ranmoor route. (*David J. Richardson Collection*)

The same site as in the previous photograph, as it appears in July 2000. The Royal Oak which can be seen in the previous photograph, is here to the right of the Chinese Firework Company. This public house is now called The Engine. (*Paul T. Langley Welch*)

The bottom of London Road, c. 1905. (*David J. Richardson Collection*)

The bottom of London Road, July 2000. (*Paul T. Langley Welch*)

Looking from Ecclesall Road to the bottom of London Road, 13 October 1957. (*David J. Richardson Collection*)

The same view of the bottom of London Road from St Mary's Gate, July 2000. (*Paul T. Langley Welch*)

Sheffield's
Old Industrial Sites

The Meadowhall shopping complex, July 2000. (*Paul T. Langley Welch*)

Carbrook Hall & Chimney Piece

An illustration showing Carbrook Hall as it appeared in the early nineteenth century, drawn and etched by E. Blore. This historic house once stood in isolated splendour on Attercliffe Common. As steelworks and factories spread from Sheffield town centre through the Lower Don Valley, during the last 150 years or so, the once picturesque Attercliffe Common was completely transformed. (*SCL Collection*)

Carbrook Hall as it appeared in around 1890. In the late twelfth century the Blunts lived at Carbrook. During the late middle ages a fine timber-framed house was erected and in 1623 a new stone wing was added. By then a branch of the illustrious Bright family of Whirlow Hall was in residence at Carbrook. John Bright of Carbrook Hall, a Parliamentarian in the Civil War, was promoted to colonel in 1643 and made Governor of Sheffield Castle the following year. The Hall was used by the Parliamentarians during the siege of Sheffield Castle in 1644. The Brights were an influential Sheffield family and today there are many reminders of the family throughout Sheffield, not least the district known as Brightside. Onetime resident of Carbrook, Mary Bright, daughter of Thomas Bright of Carbrook Hall, married Charles 2nd Marquess of Rockingham, of Wentworth Woodhouse, near Rotherham in 1752. This much loved and respected 'Whig', was twice Prime Minister. He died in office, when he succumbed to a bad bout of influenza on 1 July 1782, at the age of fifty-two. Mary Bright's pedigree and the substantial fortune to which she was heiress had made her a suitable candidate for Lord Rockingham's hand. There were no children by the marriage and on Lord Rockingham's death his estates passed to his sister's son, William 4th Earl Fitzwilliam. These estates included the Bright Legacy (which included land and properties in Sheffield). Mary, Marchioness of Rockingham, lived until December 1804. William Charles de Meuron Wentworth-Fitzwilliam, 7th Earl Fitzwilliam, was Lord Mayor of Sheffield in 1909. Streets in Sheffield bear both the Rockingham and Fitzwilliam names. A descendant of the Bright's, Admiral Southerton, sold the Carbrook Hall estate in 1819. The timber framed portion of the Hall had been demolished in about 1800. By 1855 Carbrook Hall itself had become a public house, its former estate having rapidly developed into the heart of the world's premier steel-making centre. Now most of the steelworks have gone. Carbrook Hall's nearest neighbour of any size is Meadowhall shopping complex. Carbrook Hall is still a public house today (see page 107). Although it has changed substantially in its outward appearance, this magnificent old house contains impressive interiors. It is listed Grade II. (*SCL Collection*)

Carbrook Hall, July 2000.
(*Paul T. Langley Welch*)

The Dannemora Steel Works, one of the many steelworks which were built right up to the banks of the River Don, *c.* 1900. (*David J. Richardson Collection*)

The Clyde Steelworks of Samuel Osbourne and Co. Ltd, on the banks of the River Don, *c.* 1900, a major employer of the time. The steelworks were situated between the Wicker and the River Don. The Royal Victoria Hotel can be seen on the right. Osbourne's closed in the 1970s. (*David J. Richardson Collection*)

Jack Carl drystone grinding at J. Eliot and Sons, cutlers, Sylvester Street, 1981. (*SCL Collection*)

J. Elliott and Sons: Mrs Gill is operating the pulling on machine. (*SCL Collection*)

St Philip's churchyard, Infirmary Road, *c.* 1965. The imposing building in the background is the Globe Works, the scene of several nineteenth-century trade union outrages. The musical play *The Stirrings in Sheffield*, originally produced at Sheffield Playhouse in 1966, gives an interesting and entertaining account of this troublesome period of Sheffield's industrial past. (*SCL Collection*)

The Globe Works, July 2000.
(*Paul T. Langley Welch*)

This view, taken from Rutland Road on 28 June 1965, shows several of Sheffield's vanished steelworks. (*SCL Collection*)

A view of the River Don, taken from Corporation Street Bridge in June 1965. (*SCL Collection*)

A Sheffield tinker, rather grandly calling himself a cutler, photographed just after the Second World War. (*C.H. Lea/SCL Collection*)

The River Don from Lady's Bridge, 10 January 1990. Part of the Exchange Brewery can be seen on the left. (*SCL Collection*)

The inspection department at Hiram Wild, Central Works, Herries Road, May 1997. (*SCL Collection*)

George Bradley at work, June 1997. He is forming handles at Nickel Blanks Co. Ltd, Smithfield. (*SCL Collection*)

The premises of the famous Sheffield company Henderson's, situated on the corner of Leavygreave Road and Upper Hanover Street, 1998. Henry Henderson opened his business in Broad Lane in the closing years of the nineteenth century. The firm have been producing their celebrated Henderson's Relish within a half-mile radius of the original factory ever since. A move to more modern premises, is now on the cards. Fortunately, the firm are looking for suitable premises within Sheffield, so this popular Sheffield product will continue its association with the city. Rumours of the firms imminent move have prompted some Sheffielders to stockpile bottles of the relish as a safeguard. Relish of all kinds was very popular during the late Victorian period, particularly in Yorkshire. Most firms who produced it have long since disappeared, or have been incorporated into other companies, their products being made to original recipes, far away from where the products were first conceived. (*SCL Collection*)

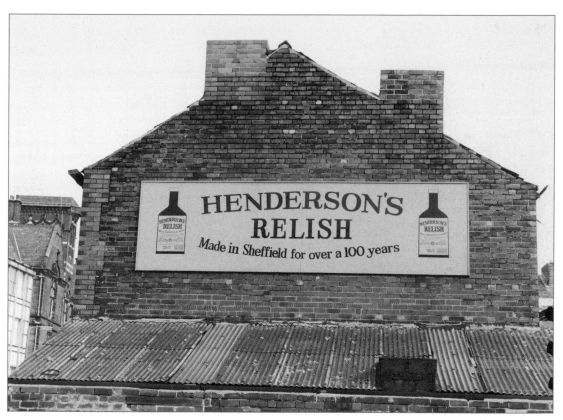

The advertising sign which adorns the gable of Henderson's factory, 1998. In its early days Henderson's Relish developed a reputation for its medicinal properties, which increased sales. The bottle in which the relish is sold has remained largely unchanged over the years; only the size has varied. The clear bottles, with their long, thin necks and bright orange labels, filled with a dark aromatic liquid, once had red or orange tops. The tops now incorporate handy shakers. The very first bottles would have been stoppered with corks sealed with wax. Henry Henderson could never have envisaged that his relish would one day cross the globe in the baggage of some of Sheffield's famous sons. Pop stars who hail from Sheffield and other celebrities have openly admitted that a bottle of it goes with them on their travels. Three-quarters of a million bottles are sold each year in Yorkshire alone. It is exported elsewhere, but is surprisingly not very popular in nearby Barnsley. Perhaps the residents there are jealous of its success? Recently a brand new product has been launched in conjunction with the publishers D.C. Thompson, famous for their children's comics *The Dandy* and *The Beano*, among others. Aimed at attracting younger customers, this new recipe for Desperate Dan Spicy Tomato Splash, is kept just as secret as that for Henderson's Relish. Perhaps that too will be just as popular as Henderson's Relish itself in another hundred years. (*SCL Collection*)

Advertisement for the Brightside and Carbrook Co-operative Society Limited. Note the unusual use of Lim, for Limited. The usual form is to use the word Limited in its entirety or, alternatively, use the abbreviation Ltd. The B & C Co-operative Society Limited was incorporated by Act of Parliament in 1868. The Central Stores, featured in this advertisement, contained the offices for the society, the entrance to which can be seen adjacent to the gates, left of the Drapery Department. The gates allowed access to the loading bay. (*SCL Collection*)

Acknowledgements

Thanks are due to the following individuals and organisations for their assistance during the production of this book.

My personal assistant Mr John D. Murray, Mr Paul T. Langley Welch, for his patience and perseverance, Mr David J. Richardson, for use of his extensive photographic collection, Mr Doug Hindmarch, Senior Local Studies Librarian at Sheffield Central Library and Mr Mike Spick and the staff of Sheffield Central Library Local Studies Department, Mr Herbert and Mrs Doreen Howse of Berdor House, Hoyland, Mr Clifford and Mrs Margaret Willoughby, Mr David Walker and Mrs Christine Walker of Walkers Newsagents, Hoyland, Miss Suki B. Walker, Mr J.H. Turner, Miss Tracy P. Deller, Miss Joanna C. Murray Deller, Ricki S. Deller, Mrs Sylvia Steel, Julie Wiggett, David Thompson and Martin Baillie; a special thank you to Tony Briggs of Harvey and Richardson, Hoyland, Mr Simon Fletcher, Annabel Fearnley, Fiona Eadie, Olwen Greany, Anne Bennett and the people of Sheffield who have offered encouragement and assistance, when I have asked for it.

Paul T. Langley Welch, who took the present-day photographs of Sheffield included in this book, works as a freelance commercial and theatrical photographer. Since 1983 he has been working for such companies as the National Theatre, the Old Vic and the Royal Shakespeare Company. Commercial clients include United Distillers, the National Tourist Board, the Arts Council of Great Britain, British Telecom, and F1 Racing (Silverstone). He has also produced films in conjunction with Pauline Turner for PPM Productions, for the National Tourist Board. In 1999 he photographed contemporary images for Geoffrey Howse's *Around Hoyland* and *A Century of Sheffield*.